outside the lines

t. kilgore splake

HAWAKAL

HAWAKAL

Published by Hawakal Publishers
185 Kali Temple Road, Nimta, Kolkata 700049
India

Email info@hawakal.com
Website www.hawakal.com

First edition June, 2019 (Paperback)

Copyright © T. Kilgore Splake 2019

Cover concept & design: Bitan Chakraborty

All rights reserved. No part of this publication may be reproduced or transmitted (other than for purposes of review/critique) in any form or by any means, electronic or mechanical, including photocopy, recording, or any information storage and retrieval system without prior permission in writing from the publisher or the copyright holder where applicable. The author asserts his moral right to be identified as the author of his work.

ISBN: 978-93-87883-66-6

Price: USD 8.99

Celebrating Autonomy

In *outside the lines*, poet t. kilgore splake strikes at the meaning of reality by exposing its rich underbelly of carnality, violence, drunkenness, despair, and forgetfulness. These poems are part autobiography, expressing the poet's doubt's and concerns while jubilating at each prospect in life. splake makes it clear that his life is full of downturns. He tells us his stubbornness is what makes him rich.

    These poems go beyond these tropes, however, into a world beyond the world. We see Man's struggle with Nature, man's struggle with woman, death of great men such as Leonard Cohen in their last breaths, suicide and health concerns, rehab, and the jealousy of others as well as personal jealousy. splake tells more in this collection than in his previous collections about what drives him as a poet and human in the wild. He unveils in poetic fashion the ability of the writer to undercut reality, to draw "outside the lines" and face what lies beyond—those lines that "show, don't tell", in the author's vernacular. So much is behind the world we take for granted. What moves it, makes it grow? These poems suggest internal struggle is a powerful medium for motivating oneself. Even though we destroy Nature, she ultimately wins. What lesson is learned? Is immortality merely a state of being? Is it wisdom of some kind?

Some people live the standard life. Others look at the ones who are going beyond. Even though a visionary appears mad, he or she is the driving wedge between what we see and what we know. Those who brave the wilderness will find new heart in its mystery.

This collection is one of the most interesting and revealing of splake's works I have read for all of the above reasons. "Outside the lines" is a metaphor for death, for struggle to exist, for looking and living beyond the normal. The book is carefully structured in splake's idiosyncratic style of centered impressionistic lines that speak for themselves. He is part beatnik, part Transcendentalist. The reader will find this collection to be unusual in its own right, but will not find it unfamiliar if he or she has read other splake books.

In his life as writer and poet, t. kilgore splake has acted as historian, naturalist, photographer, and poet simultaneously. "outside the lines" combines all these roles into one convincing and beautiful work celebrating the autonomy of the human soul.

Dustin Pickering
Publisher and Editor
at *Transcendent Zero Press*

Contents

understanding	11
morning hello	12
light my fire	13
freedom	14
moving beyond	15
awakening	16
becoming	17
untitled	18
seeing clearly	19
saving the wilderness	20
poet's new life	21
rat bastard time	22
in the beginning	23
silent appreciation	24
survival	25
home	26
lie	27
going to fly	28
literary vision	29
peace	30
mad dream fevers	31
nada mas	32

murder	33
amen amen	34
night into morning	35
winter	36
eyes wide shut	37
wealth	38
writing wisdom	39
beyond autumn light	40
graybeard memories	41
answer for critic	42
escape	43
long white finis	44
no exit	45
aching heart	46
out of nowhere	47
eyes wide open	48
vision from above	49
bardic musing	50
voyeur's understanding	51
escape	52
what lies beyond	53
you're all over blue	54
what do you want	55
poet's journey	56
solitude	57
outside the lines	59
last will and testament	61
one more once	63

understanding

walden pond wisdom
thoreau's beliefs
ignore others 'musts'
government demands

morning hello

barista's message
coffee house napkin
cold cozy nights
under warm blanket
hot espresso surprise

light my fire

poet's soul rising
beyond campfire ashes
like jim morrison's
pere lachaise ghosts
wisdom everywhere

freedom

"leaves of grass"
walt's powerful visions
able to live
beyond others rules
free butterfly floating
over society

moving beyond

cell phone technology
deny creative challenges
risking new adventures
try shot of jack
cold beer chaser
taste of life's reality

awakening

cold night winds
sweeping clouds across sky
poet's ashes rising
disappearing into heaven
bright flickering stardust
lighting the world

becoming

dark late night
stars light reflecting
off black river currents
quietly moving beyond
after first dawn
disappearing into morning

untitled

cool light breeze
pine trees humming
dry twigs burning
inside fire ring
poems rising
heading to heaven

seeing clearly

lange's wpa photograph
migrant mother holding child
dreams long forgotten
like bruegel's peasant
woman staring at heaven
knowing rainbow not there

saving the wilderness

greedy people
owning cliffs
brautigan creek
thimbleberry bushes
distant god angry
over man's destroying
nature's peace

poet's new life

waking early morning
exploding hangover pains
cold delicatessen chicken
warm tab cola
car stuck in snowbank
first day of retirement
brain quietly whispering
"you are free"

rat bastard time

moving down birth canal
doctor slapping bottom
breathing first breath
time rapidly flying by
enjoying good times
surviving life's setbacks
suddenly old man
looking for lost keys

in the beginning

strayed off path
lost in puckerbrush
thickets of branches
wet decaying humus
no animal signs
evidence of native life
finding earth as it was
first day of creation

silent appreciation

early morning light
brautigan creek shadows
light mist falling
enjoying silent beauty
not necessary to thank
holy book scriptures
pray to stone gods
for wilderness pleasure

survival

dark nostrils flared
hungry eyes gleaming
teeth and claws
seizing captured prey
silent song of bones
wilderness wolf
lives another day

home

winter snowshoe print
spring crocus buds
thunderstorms in july
autumn leaves coloring
changing seasons
bring poet closer to earth
touching powers that be

lie

church basement meeting
regular night greeting
steady voice saying
"i'm tom an alcoholic"
while angry brain screams
denying the words
poet still searching
seeking his soul

going to fly

late moonless night
headlights off
motorcycle past red line
cylinders exploding
shaking tree leaves
highway miles disappearing
poet soon reaching
dark side of the moon

literary vision

hungry young artist
disappearing into himself
spending long quiet hours
creating masterwork
serious important story
words living beyond him
influencing others thinking
from cradle to grave

peace

watching sunset
lean-to shelter
beside brautigan creek
poet enjoying
soft flowing melodies
forest slowly darkening
waiting night whispers
as brother richard says
simple as that

mad dream fevers

waking early morning
loud thunderstorm noise
bright lightning flashes
illuminating paula's face
haunting mirror reflections
like rita and orson
"lady from shanghai"
freezing our love
stopping the heart

nada mas

owning several cameras
expensive filming accessories
understanding f-stops
bracketing subjects
depth of field dimensions
lacking creative vision
determined artistic drive
photographer never
seeing real picture

murder

iv disconnected
no more dripping
dope killing pain
machine turned off
silencing beepings
mechanical pulse
choosing suicide
over vegetable existence
or nursing home hell

amen amen

after last call
closing time again
killing tavern neon
stacking up chairs
wiping down bar
jukebox silent
sad lonely man
leaving alone
like johnny cash song
leoarnd cohen poem

night into morning

riding on empty

turning tranny miles
tunnel vision stare
mindless distractions
lost in radio noise
programmed pop songs
repetitive inane lyrics
thumbing text message
sharing emotional feelings
painful broken heart
with someone not caring

winter

tiny snowflake
melting on tongue
bringing warm memories
cross-country skiing
ice hockey games
frozen mill pond ice
skating with alison
holding her close
tender young times
living the moment

eyes wide shut

sad young girl
black empty despair
lost in deep depression
wildly crying
"bury me bury me"
conscious moments
thinking escape pain
razor blade
bottles of pills
pulling gun trigger

wealth

wild berry feast
pine needle aromas
spring wildflower beauty
summer thunderstorm
licking wet rain
off tender leaves
listening to birdsongs
owl's evening greetings
wilderness poet
very rich man

writing wisdom

poems and stories
experimental works
disturbing readers
rejected by editors
dangerous creative voice
joining past writers
jack and allen
beatnik rebels
whispering from shadows
there is another way

beyond autumn light

soft evening breeze
pine needle hum
brautigan creek currents
happy wet melody
cliffs wilderness deer
dark ghostly companions
poet's silent shadow
rising in mists
soul leaving earth
moving toward heaven

graybeard memories

pre-google times
when reading was fun
page turning adventures
exciting heroic tales
before underlining
saving notes in folder
for later contesting
 elusive dame muse
after writing day
pabst good company

answer for critic

writing same poem
over and again
feels so good
like jacking off
watching naked women
computer porn site
or warm memories
of fucking wives
time when poet
believed in love

escape

another writing morning
contesting elusive muse
wildly scribbling
words filling page
poet remembering
endless days
prisoner of job
long lonely nights
sliding into boozy sleep
praying for freedom
precious rat bastard time

long white finis

beyond canadian storms
snow crunching under boots
spring energy happening
under white drifts
mice families growing
small eggs warming
soon new life
bird nest homes
poet waiting ice out
smell it breathe it
coming into spring

no exit

blades of green grass
protruding through concrete
empty highways
no travelers passing
traffic light
dark and unblinking
hanging on single cable
swaying in breeze
on the road miles
leading nowhere
mother nature always wins

aching heart

besides trout fishing
wrestling poems
contesting elusive muse
missing my daughters
robin and casey
almost young athena
now grown women
living in parts distant
reminding me
of papa hem and renata
lonely old graybeard
still hungry for love

out of nowhere

quiet dementia
smothering artist's life
no longer remembering
taking medicine
paying bills
putting garbage curbside
setting bedroom alarm
"where's my cell phone"
however studio hours
as potter wheel turns
shaping wet clay
creative magic
still in his hands

eyes wide open

rotting in earth
buried in black hole
not abandoned casket
ashes floating
carried by winds
over wildflowers
beyond forest trees
flying with birds
of soft melodies
leaving behind
brook trout friends
pleasant memories
brautigan creek days

vision from above

late night hours
dark ghostly shadow
final odyssey
floating along cliffs trail
stars lighting path
rising to summit
surveying earth
from escarpment edge
missing tomorrow
no more future
life now finished
regretting unwritten poems
other creations not done
artist quickly forgotten

bardic musing

one-room apartment
little excess baggage
no refrigerator
single burner hotplate
small space heater
sleeping bag and futon
dollar store telephone
bathroom down the hall
late night hours
sipping green tea
feeling burning desires
lonely starving poet
praying work discovered
waiting waiting

voyeur's understanding

almost naked woman
sliding down pole
wiggling her flesh
dance floor gyrations
knowing better
to put dollars in her thong
young midwestern boy
wise to county fair games
trying to win prizes
inside claw machine
crane's metal teeth
dropping valuable things
quickly learning
house and women
always win

escape

tight airplane row
automobile seat
small cubicle desk
cell iron bars
hard church pew
close isolation
without taste of freedom
instead find reality
escaping in wilderness
hiking forest trails
smelling wildflowers
dark exotic fragrance
dancing with butterflies
eating ripe berries
resting beside stream
momentarily lost
enjoying soft melodies

what lies beyond

young girl poet
seeking her voice
in love with painter
boyfriend's canvas
splashes of oily colors
living together
sharing creative energies
like carver and tess
sylvia and hughes
starving artist companions
passions still strong
after long life together
through passing years
helping each other
understand death
face new reality
what lies beyond

you're all over blue

rosetta café waitress
stone washed jeans
thick navy wool sweater
young barista's reply
"no, not really
self-absorbed response
girl having bad day
drinking morning espresso
thinking she should know
big mama thornton
bessie smith
sad suffering women
hard painful lives
always begging others
blues rising
from deep in their souls
soft sweet hallelujahs
floating to heaven

what do you want

my wife asked me
one hot july afternoon
after deciding
not to buy old delivery van
burnt out professor
marriage in trouble
later becoming farmer
raising cattle and pigs
huge vegetable garden
serious drinking problem
three rehab failures
one-and-a-half
suicide attempts
when early one morning
hungover in the woods
writing word on paper
and then another one
suddenly having a poem
answer for ex-wife

poet's journey

from greenwich village
to europe by boat
tramp steamer cabin
old paris hotel room
accordion elevator door
french riviera
antibbes and cannes
italian seaports
visiting roman ruins
tasting la dolce vita
on to greek islands
renting hydra cottage
eating fresh feta
drinking retsina
remote local tavern
hidden in olive grove
dreaming of leonard cohen
marvelous creative wisdom
singing sad ballads
before becoming darker
his spirit drifting away

solitude

crowded paris cafes
community of other artists
pretenders always talking
never creating new works
escaping like paul gaugin
fleeing loud nervous city
quiet distant place
with forest trees
rocky granite cliffs
ruins with history
time had passed by
remote wilderness streams
tiny waterfalls
tilled farm fields
waiting autumn harvest
near large body of water
sea or inland lake
endless clear sky
amazing new light

releasing creative energies
painter slowly becoming
one with nature
moving closer to god

outside the lines

sister's coloring book
crayon drawings precise
her reality inside the lines
later chasing academic success
doctoral dissertation
inside fancy leather box
pride of family reunions
mary successful
making something of herself
professor seeking grants
attending special workshops
working on new book
while younger brother
moving past boundaries
rebelling against rules
creative imagination
exploring beauty
touching naked intimacy
dancing with life

writing poems
with words that sing
jealous others watching
eager to do the same
practical and cautious
chickenshit to try

last will and testament

graybeard memories
waiting modest inheritance
after aging mother passes
often reading classifieds
automobile dealer listings
checking pickup truck prices
yet after margaret's death
receiving my share
sudden new wealth
didn't feel like mine
recalling my youth
post depression childhood
always earning and saving
for things desired
faithfully saving coins
to purchase new bike
buying black beret
deserved recognition
of becoming a poet

now no ex-wives
serious lady friends
children long estranged
living who knows where
seriously wondering
who should benefit
from mother's dollars
county animal shelter
alcoholics anonymous
generous donation
buying christmas toys
back to school backpacks
caring fifth street angels
"new becoming mission"

one more once

exhausted photographer
dropping camera and tripod
collapsing in woods
back against tree
surveying the forest
suddenly able to see
cycle of life's mystery
without good or evil
happiness or misery
busy communities
beetles and earthworms
worker ants foraging
lichen living on bark
microbes turning wilderness
into fertile soil
for new things to grow
besides forest evolution
necessary animal survival
furry and feathered creatures

bloody talons sharp claws
daily seeking prey
for continued existence
surrounded by music
trees lightly singing
mid-afternoon breeze
wet soft melodies
streams flowing water
wild birdsongs
soon decision to make
like beaten fighter
stay on canvas
taking the count
resting in moon shadows
until early dawn
then disappearing
like shadowy ghost
floating into mist
or dusting ass off
getting back up
continue the punishment
bravely surviving
part of the world

www.ingramcontent.com/pod-product-compliance
Lightning Source LLC
Chambersburg PA
CBHW031502040426
42444CB00007B/1175